Beauty and the Beast

Many years ago, there lived a merchant who had three daughters and four sons. With the absence of their mother, the merchant spoilt his daughters a lot, except Beauty, who was a sweet-natured girl, refusing all expensive gifts. You see, she wanted to save her father's money as the other two had long lists of fine items they wanted. Beauty was happy with less and would take care of the house while the rest enjoyed the luxuries of fine living.

As time passed, the merchant lost his business. They transferred to a small country home. Beauty worked even harder but the rest did not move a finger. The merchant had to go to work yet again. All the children had grand lists they gave. Beauty had none but she did not want to make her sisters look bad, and so asked for a rose!

The merchant did not get much business. He was on his way back when he saw a grand castle. On the castle grounds, he spotted some beautiful roses in full bloom. He plucked one. Instantly, he heard a bellowing voice from behind. It was a mighty, ugly looking beast!

The Beast held him prisoner in his castle. He came to know of the merchant's daughters and made an offer. He would exchange him for one of his daughters. The Beast sent him home with a chest of gold and made a threat that he would only wait a few days for either the merchant, or one of his daughters, to come to the castle on their own.

On reaching home, the merchant shared his problem with his children. He was the breadwinner for the family. The two daughters refused, but Beauty was happy to go as long as the family was safe and well provided for.

The father had no choice but to let Beauty go. He was heartbroken when Beauty left, even though the Beast had treated him well. Beauty reached the castle and entered the hall in time for supper. There was a grand meal laid and the Beast announced his arrival with a loud growl.

'You are mine and shall remain here forever. You may use and ask for anything you like for it is all yours, but you may never leave the castle.' Beauty was scared initially, but in a few weeks, she saw the kindness and sensitivity with which the Beast took care of her.

One night, while sleeping in her luxurious bedroom, she had a nightmare that her father was ill with grief, worrying about her. The Beast decided she must go home even though he had become very fond of Beauty and knew he could not live without her. Yet, he could not see Beauty unhappy.

Beauty reached home. Her father recovered, knowing she was treated well. Her sisters were happy as they could now use her expensive items. But the moment they tried to reach out to one of her objects, it would disappear and would only be seen when Beauty needed it. The Beast had ensured she never wanted a thing!

Beauty had another nightmare that her Beast was dying. She could not wait and rode swiftly in a carriage to the castle. As she entered the castle grounds, she saw the Beast lying close to her favourite rose bushes, dead!

In despair, as she cried her heart out, she held him close and openly declared her love for him. The tears fell on the mighty Beast and he came alive, transforming into a prince. He held Beauty and told her how a witch had cursed him, from which only true love could set him free.

The castle came alive with love and laughter as the courtiers and loyal subjects returned. Beauty and the Beast, now a handsome prince, married and lived happily ever after!